VOICES on the WIND

And My Heart Soars

The beauty of the trees,
The softness of the air,
The fragrance of the grass,
   speaks to me.

The summit of the mountain,
The thunder of the sky,
The rhythm of the sea,
   speaks to me.

The faintness of the stars,
The freshness of the morning,
The dew drop on the flower,
   speaks to me.

The strength of fire,
The taste of salmon,
The trail of the sun,
And the life that never goes away,
   They speak to me.

And my heart soars.

Chief Dan George

VOICES on the WIND

Poems for All Seasons

Selected by

DAVID BOOTH

Illustrated by

MICHÈLE LEMIEUX

Morrow Junior Books / New York

For Emilie and Mathieu

M.L.

To Jay

D.B.

First United States edition published 1990.
Co-published with Kids Can Press Ltd., Toronto, Canada.
Some illustrations published in Germany by Otto Maier Verlag in the title Lieder von der Natur.

Compilation copyright © 1990 by David Booth
Illustrations copyright © 1990 by Ravensburger Buchverlag
Permission acknowledgments appear on pages 40 and 41,
which constitute a continuation
of the copyright page.

Printed in the United States of America.
1   2   3   4   5   6   7   8   9   10
Library of Congress Cataloging-in-Publication Data
Voices on the wind : poems for all seasons / selected by David Booth ; illustrated by Michèle Lemieux.
p.   cm.
Summary: An anthology of poems celebrating the sights and sounds of the four seasons.
ISBN 0-688-09554-2. —ISBN 0-688-9555-0 (lib. bdg.)
1. Seasons—Juvenile literature. 2. Nature—Juvenile literature.
3. Children's poetry, American. 4. Children's poetry, English.
[1. Seasons—Poetry. 2. Nature—Poetry. 3. American poetry—
Collections. 4. English poetry—Collections.] I. Booth, David. II. Lemieux, Michèle, ill.
PS595.S42V6   1990   811.008'036—dc20   90-5566   CIP   AC

Contents

WHO AM I?

The trees ask me,
And the sky,
And the sea asks me
      Who am I?

The grass asks me,
And the sand,
And the rocks ask me
      Who I am.

The wind tells me
At nightfall,
And the rain tells me
     Someone small.

    Someone small
    Someone small
    But a piece
         of
         it
     all.

    Felice Holman

GOOD MORNING

Good morning to the great trees
That bend above this little house;
Good morning to the wind that comes
And goes among the leaves, and sings;
Good morning to the birds, the grass,
Good morning to the bare ground;
Good morning, pond across the way
That must have opened both its eyes;
Good morning, everything that shines
Or doesn't shine; good morning, mole
And worm and nesting mouse—good morning,
Morning to all things that ever
Were and will be, and that are.

Mark Van Doren

AND SUDDENLY SPRING

The winds of March were sleeping.
I hardly felt a thing.
The trees were standing quietly.
It didn't seem like spring.
Then suddenly the winds awoke
And raced across the sky.
They bumped right into April,
Splashing springtime in my eye.

Margaret Hillert

LITTLE SEEDS

Little seeds we sow in spring,
Growing while the robins sing,
Give us carrots, peas and beans,
Tomatoes, pumpkins, squash and greens.

And we pick them,
One and all,
Through the summer,
Through the fall.

Winter comes, then spring, and then
Little seeds we sow again.

Else Holmelund Minarik

BOUQUET

In Goldie's garden,
Flowers grow
Within a neat
And ordered row.

But in our woodland,
Never neat,
Grow jumbled rose
And meadowsweet,

And lily bell
And Queen Anne's lace
And dandelions
Everyplace.

Now, I prefer
The wildness where
The flowers have
To give and share.

But Goldie says
Both things are good:
The well-kept garden
And the wood.

Jane Yolen

11

ODE TO SPRING

O spring, O spring,
You wonderful thing!
O spring, O spring, O spring!
O spring, O spring,
When the birdies sing
I feel like a king,
    O spring!

Walter R. Brooks

TREES

Trees are the kindest things I know,
They do no harm, they simply grow

And spread a shade for sleepy cows,
And gather birds among their boughs.

They give us fruit in leaves above,
And wood to make our houses of,

And leaves to burn on Hallowe'en,
And in the spring new buds of green.

They are the first when day's begun
To touch the beams of morning sun,

They are the last to hold the light
When evening changes into night,

And when a moon floats on the sky,
They hum a drowsy lullaby

Of sleepy children long ago . . .
Trees are the kindest things I know.

Harry Behn

A LITTLE SONG OF LIFE

Glad that I live am I;
That the sky is blue;
Glad for the country lanes,
And the fall of dew.

After the sun the rain;
After the rain the sun;
This is the way of life,
Till the work be done.

All that we need to do,
Be we low or high,
Is to see that we grow
Nearer the sky.

Lizette Woodworth Reese

THAT WAS SUMMER

Have you ever smelled summer?
Sure you have.
Remember that time
When you were tired of running
Or doing nothing much
And you were hot
And you flopped right down on the ground?
Remember how the warm soil smelled—
And the grass?
That was summer.

Remember that time
When the storm blew up quick
And you stood under a ledge
And watched the rain till it stopped
And when it stopped
You walked out again to the sidewalk,
The quiet sidewalk?
Remember how the pavement smelled—
All steamy warm and wet?
That was summer.

Remember that time
When you were trying to climb
Higher in the tree
And you didn't know how
And your foot was hurting in the fork
But you were holding tight
To the branch?
Remember how the bark smelled then—
All dusty dry, but nice?
That was summer.

If you try very hard,
Can you remember that time
When you played outside all day
And you came home for dinner
And had to take a bath right away,
Right away?
It took you a long time to pull
Your shirt over your head.
Do you remember smelling the sunshine?
That was summer.

Marci Ridlon

16

THE FIELD MOUSE

I live among the grasses,
   And watch them growing high,
And as the summer passes
   They seem to touch the sky.

The Spiders are my neighbors,
   Busy people they,
I watch them at their labors,
   Spinning day by day.

The Earwig comes a-calling,
   The Ladybird as well,
And Snails go slowly crawling,
   And Slugs, without a shell.

The Bumble, fat and furry,
   A flying visit pays,
And Caterpillars hurry
   Adown the grassy ways.

I am your little brother,
   A Mouse in brown and gray,
So if we meet each other,
   Please let me run away!

Enid Blyton

BROWNY BEE

Little Mr. Browny Bee,
Gather honey for my tea;
Come into my garden, do,
I've every kind of flower for you.

There's blossom on my tiny tree,
And daisies in the grass you'll see;
There's lavender, and scented stocks,
And rows of frilly hollyhocks.

I've marigolds, and pansies too,
And Canterbury bells of blue;
There's rosemary, and scented thyme,
And foxglove heads you'll love to climb.

I've gilly flowers, and roses red,
All waiting in my garden bed;
Seek honey where my flowers are
To fill my little honey jar.

Irene F. Pawsey

DOWN DIP THE BRANCHES

Down dip the branches,
The long leafy branches,
Down dip the branches
To bring old robin in.

Underneath the haytops,
The warm windy haytops,
Underneath the haytops
The mice are creeping home.

Soon it will be sunset,
Red and yellow sunset,
Soon it will be sunset,
With everything indoors.

Apples for supper.
Sing, sing for supper.
After, after supper,
Sing awhile in bed.

Mouse in the meadow,
The green sleepy meadow,
Mouse in the meadow,
Fold your little paws.

Robin in the branches,
The dark sleepy branches,
Old robin in the branches,
Shut, shut, shut your eyes.

Mark Van Doren

CONVERSATION

Mousie, mousie,
Where is your little wee housie?
  Here is the door,
  Under the floor,
    Said mousie, mousie.

Mousie, mousie,
May I come into your housie?
  You can't get in,
  You have to be thin,
    Said mousie, mousie.

Mousie, mousie,
Won't you come out of your housie?
  I'm sorry to say
  I'm busy all day,
    Said mousie, mousie.

Rose Fyleman

RAIN SIZES

Rain comes in various sizes.
Some rain is as small as a mist.
It tickles your face with surprises,
And tingles as if you'd been kissed.

Some rain is the size of a sprinkle
And doesn't put out all the sun.
You can see the drops sparkle and twinkle,
And a rainbow comes out when it's done.

Some rain is as big as a nickel
And comes with a crash and a hiss.
It comes down too heavy to tickle.
It's more like a splash than a kiss.

When it rains the right size and you're wrapped in
Your rainclothes, it's fun out of doors.
But run home before you get trapped in
The big rain that rattles and roars.

John Ciardi

THE LAMB

Little lamb, who made thee?
Dost thou know who made thee,
Gave thee life and made thee feed
By the stream and o'er the mead;
Gave thee clothing of delight,
Softest clothing, woolly, bright?
Gave thee such a tender voice,
Making all the vales rejoice?
Little lamb, who made thee?
Dost thou know who made thee?

Little lamb, I'll tell thee,
Little lamb, I'll tell thee!
He is called by thy name,
For He calls Himself a lamb.
He is meek, and He is mild;
He became a little child.
I a child, and thou a lamb,
We are called by His name.
Little lamb, God bless thee.
Little lamb, God bless thee.

William Blake

AUTUMN WOODS

I like the woods
        In autumn
When dry leaves hide the ground,
When the trees are bare
And the wind sweeps by
With a lonesome rushing sound.

I can rustle the leaves
        In autumn
And I can make a bed
In the thick dry leaves
That have fallen
From the bare trees
Overhead.

James S. Tippett

FISHES COME BITE!

Fishes come bite!
Fishes come bite!
I have fished all day;
I will fish all night.
I sit in the rain on my lily-leaf boat,
But never a minnow will bob my float.
Fishes come bite!

Beatrix Potter

AUTUMN FIRES

In the other gardens
   And all up the vale,
From the autumn bonfires
   See the smoke trail!

Pleasant summer over
   And all the summer flowers,
The red fire blazes,
   The gray smoke towers.

Sing a song of seasons!
   Something bright in all!
Flowers in the summer,
   Fires in the fall!

Robert Louis Stevenson

TAKING OFF

The airplane taxis down the field
And heads into the breeze,
It lifts its wheels above the ground,
It skims above the trees,
It rises high and higher
Away up toward the sun,
It's just a speck against the sky
—And now it's gone!

Mary McB. Green

WHO HAS SEEN THE WIND?

Who has seen the wind?
  Neither I nor you:
But when the leaves hang trembling
  The wind is passing through.

Who has seen the wind?
  Neither you nor I:
But when the trees bow down their heads
  The wind is passing by.

Christina Rossetti

LADYBIRD! LADYBIRD!

Ladybird! Ladybird! Fly away home,
Night is approaching, and sunset is come:
The herons are flown to their trees by the Hall;
Felt, but unseen, the damp dewdrops fall.
This is the close of a still summer day;
Ladybird! Ladybird! haste! fly away!

Emily Brontë

UNDER THE GROUND

What is under the grass,
Way down in the ground,
Where everything is cool and wet
With darkness all around?

Little pink worms live there;
Ants and brown bugs creep
Softly round the stones and rocks
Where roots are pushing deep.

Do they hear us walking
On the grass above their heads;
Hear us running over
While they snuggle in their beds?

Rhoda W. Bacmeister

SPIDERS

Spiders seldom see too well.
Spiders have no sense of smell.
Spiders spin out silken threads.
Spiders don't have separate heads.
Spider bodies are two-part.
Spider webs are works of art.
Spiders don't have any wings.
Spiders live on living things.
Spiders always have eight legs.
Spiders hatch straight out of eggs.
Since all these facts are surely so,
Spiders are not insects, no!

Mary Ann Hoberman

GO WIND

Go wind, blow
Push wind, swoosh.
    Shake things
    take things
    make things
        fly.

    Ring things
    swing things
    fling things
        high.

Go wind, blow
Push things
wheee.
    No, wind, no.
    Not me—
    not *me.*

    Lilian Moore

WHITE FIELDS

In the wintertime we go
Walking in the fields of snow;

Where there is no grass at all;
Where the top of every wall,

Every fence and every tree,
Is as white as white can be.

Pointing out the way we came,
Every one of them the same—

All across the fields there be
Prints in silver filigree;

And our mothers always know,
By the footprints in the snow,

Where it is the children go.

James Stephens

I AM FLYING!

I am flying! I am flying!
I am riding on the breeze,
I am soaring over meadows,
I am sailing over seas,
I ascend above the cities
Where the people, small as ants,
Cannot sense the keen precision
Of my aerobatic dance.

I am flying! I am flying!
I am climbing unconfined,
I am swifter than the falcon,
And I leave the wind behind,
I am swooping, I am swirling
In a jubilant display,
I am brilliant as a comet
Blazing through the Milky Way.

I am flying! I am flying!
I am higher than the moon,
Still, I think I'd best be landing,
And it cannot be too soon,
For some nasty information
Has lit up my little brain—
I am flying! I am flying!
But I fly without a plane.

Jack Prelutsky

37

A FOOTPRINT ON THE AIR

"Stay!" said the child. The bird said, "No,
My wing has mended, I must go.
I shall come back to see you though,
One night, one day—"

                       "How shall I know?"
"Look for my footprint in the snow."

"The snow soon goes—oh, that's not fair!"
"Don't grieve. Don't grieve. I shall be there
In the bright season of the year,
One night, one day—"

                       "But tell me, where?"
"Look for my footprint on the air."

Naomi Lewis